BEHIND THE SHIELD OF A STRONG FAÇADE

A suicidal crisis

Christine Dodson

Published in Australia by Sid Harta Books & Print Pty Ltd,
ABN: 34632585293
23 Stirling Crescent, Glen Waverley, Victoria 3150 Australia
Telephone: +61 3 9560 9920, Facsimile: +61 3 9545 1742
E-mail: author@sidharta.com.au

First published in Australia 2023
This edition published 2023
Copyright © Christine Dodson 2023
Cover design, typesetting: WorkingType (www.workingtype.com.au)

The right of Christine Dodson to be identified as the
Author of the Work has been asserted in accordance with the
Copyright, Designs and Patents Act 1988.

All rights reserved. No part of this publication may be reproduced, stored in a retrieval system, or transmitted, in any form or by any means without the prior written permission of the publisher, nor be otherwise circulated in any form of binding or cover other than that in which it is published and without a similar condition being imposed on the subsequent purchaser.

ISBN: 978-1-922958-41-9

About the Author

Christine Dodson lives in Melbourne, Australia and is married with one son who has multiple disabilities. She graduated in 2006 from Monash University with a Bachelor of Arts majoring in psychology, and in 2008 she attained a Post-graduate Diploma in Psychology. She has worked as a volunteer telephone counsellor with Griefline.

Christine enjoys attending U3A classes, supporting her son's football club, visiting her elderly parents in care and exploring Jnana Yoga.

She has always enjoyed writing, finding it good therapy. This is her first book.

To all those crossing from life to death and back again, be it a near-death experience, a past-life regression, or an encounter with suicide, your experiences are real and need to be heard. This is for all those people.

ACKNOWLEDGEMENTS

Writing my story wasn't the hard bit, managing to stay alive long enough to put it down in words, that was the difficult part.

In the months prior to my suicide attempt, I put my husband through a living hell. More than once, while I was struggling with powerful waves of grief, he tried to encourage me, or say something positive to lighten my mood. Not knowing how to cope, I snapped at him often and notwithstanding the Covid lockdowns (being a Melburnian during the pandemic was not easy), also took out my frustrations on him. David you deserve a medal. Thank you.

David's positive comments on my first piece of writing about my suicide encounter, a 3000-word essay entitled, "Everything Just Felt So Heavy", also empowered me and gave me the impetus to extend on that essay and ultimately become the book you are now reading. Again, thank you.

My autistic son Jason, whom I adore, deserves a special

mention. The Covid lockdowns, with the loss of some of his routines, were incredibly difficult. Thanks to Blairlogie Living and Learning, the providers of his Day Program, who managed to stay open during these awful periods of 2020 and 2021, thus giving us a vital stress-relieving valve and allowing the retention of some sanity in the household!

Jason also had to contend with an often-strained atmosphere in the household during 2021 and 2022. He's tough though. With encouragement he can and does get through some extraordinary challenges in life. His quirky sense of humour was a light in the darkness for me in the early weeks after my attempt, and I often wondered how I would feel when he finally left home. I do miss him as he is and always will be the light of my life, but he is relaxed, settled and happy now in his group home. And I have learned to let go. Love you heaps mate.

Speaking of hard times, I've really only had two GPs in my life, two males. One literally saved my life, the other worked to prevent me from taking it. In the latter case, and just days after my attempt, I felt that he was going to take care of me. He made me feel safe. He knew that I had acted out of character and was alarmed. He was even willing to read my initial essay, as described above. I can't thank him enough for all that he has done. I have told him that he is not allowed to retire any time soon!

I can't leave off without acknowledging the important role of my therapist. It was his encouragement when, like my GP, he read my piece on 'feeling heavy', together with an older one on my IVF battles entitled, "The Gift Box of My Psyche", that made me feel like I should pursue my writing further. Once before I had tried writing a book without managing to get it published. His comment, "You have a real gift", boosted my confidence and helped to convince me to try again.

I hope the faith shown in my writing ability translates into a transformative experience for the reader. Life IS worth living. Always.

Contents

Prequel	A past life	1
Chapter 1	I was always the strong one	7
Chapter 2	When mental health issues and antidepressant withdrawal collide	29
Chapter 3	I am only one person	45
Chapter 4	Recovery from suicidality	61
Chapter 5	Therapy insights and changed spirituality	73
Endnotes		99

PREQUEL

A past life

It has happened before. Being overwhelmed and unable to continue the fight. Not being strong enough to prevent things from closing in on me. Feeling unheard. Wanting someone to care enough to want to save me. But no one did, and I succumbed to the exhaustion of the extreme circumstances. The difference between then and now is that this time, I didn't die.

I'm talking about a past life. In 1987, seeking help for the scourge of the 1980s, repetitive strain injury (RSI), I went to see a masseur. Someone had told me that this would help my wrist pain. This was pre-internet, so I looked up the Yellow Pages and contacted a local person. Initially ignoring the advertisement of metaphysical alignment and balancing, I toddled off to the first appointment.

The practitioner was an older man, and I felt comfortable

in his presence. Having long been interested in the metaphysical, the idea of a past-life regression piqued my interest, and I soon found myself back in his rooms and under hypnosis. What happened in this single hour-long session unlocked something that enabled me to make sense of my behaviours, one of which was difficulty in seeking help. At the age of just twenty-five, I'd always had difficulty telling people how I felt. It always seemed easier to withdraw to my bedroom and suffer alone. I still isolate myself when feeling wounded, thirty-five years later.

Back to the regression. I was invited to imagine myself outside, then onto the driveway next door. What did I see? Immediately, I had a sense of the Victorian gold rush era near Bendigo. I saw a dry, dusty street and horse-drawn carts plodding along. It wasn't my imagination; it had a qualitatively different feel. I was born in Melbourne in 1962, but what I was sensing, I believe, happened more than a hundred years earlier. Something profound was going on.

I was transported into a two-storey house, akin to a terrace house, and upstairs. This was my bedroom. It was sparsely furnished with just a wooden bed and chair. It was not a happy place. Somehow, I knew that my father, in this regression, was a gold-digger and a drunk. In this life, I am a female with shoulder-length, curly (permed) brown hair but now I was a boy aged about sixteen with short, blond, curly hair. I was not aware of any siblings. I was aware, though, that my mother was afraid of my father. My sense was that I tried to be the strong one and protect her. I have a mental image of her standing there in the kitchen, clasping her hands together, one hand over the other, in front of her legs. She was passive.

Again, I was transported, this time into my bedroom. My father had become violent, and I was seeking a safe haven. It didn't work: as he entered the room, he took off his belt. As he came at me, I curled up into a foetal ball on the bed and put my arms up to shield my face. It is at this point that my essence left the room. 'I' didn't want to be there. My hypnotist said that I had died. I had died from a vicious beating. No one had heard my cries. No one had tried to save me. Violence and fear were the victors. The paralysis was complete. My mother must have been frozen in her fear while I became unconscious, then lifeless. I was dead.

Back to the present. As the following chapters will reveal, the theme of not being heard has dogged me, despite my difficulty in seeking help when in need. My not being heard is hidden behind the psychological defence mechanism of projection, as will be explained later. An inability to seek help when needed is a learned method of survival in the face of horrific violence, a pattern of behaviour that now needs to be unlearned.

Additionally, and despite the deep pain of being the ultimate victim of domestic violence, I still wanted to be loved enough that someone would care enough to try to save me. When this didn't happen, I felt abandoned. In this life, I have kind and loving parents. I was raised in a warm, encouraging and safe environment. Yet echoes of this past life remain with me. I don't let anyone get too close. I want to be loved, but I don't know how.

Keeping people at arm's length prevents me from getting hurt. It's easier that way. Once before, in this life, this has translated into a lack of help-seeking that almost took my life. On a conscious level, it was unintentional. On Christmas Day 1972, I had abdominal pains on the lower right side. I told my parents that I didn't feel well. They didn't become aware of my pain for another eight hours. In hospital that night, and during the operation that ensued, my appendix ruptured and I almost died.

Thirty-plus years later, and following on from my past-life regression, echoes of that past have arisen more than once in the form of breakthrough memories and psychological insights. Yet my reluctance to open myself up, be vulnerable and seek help in the face of extraordinarily difficult and emotionally painful circumstances remains an issue.

In the following chapters, I seek to weave together the exigencies of impossible psycho-social stressors, the

PREQUEL   A past life

breakthrough insights and how my continuing reluctance to seek help led to my attempt at taking my own life.

CHAPTER 1

I was always the strong one

Mental health issues of the past

I have always been the strong one. From an early age, I was also drawn to those in emotional pain. Strange. People could ask me probing questions about myself, ones I answered despite my discomfort, but I couldn't return the favour. Being vulnerable makes people uncomfortable, and since I don't like that feeling, I also don't want that for others. Being vulnerable doesn't sit easily alongside being strong.

Retreating behind the façade of being strong, I didn't tell my parents that I was in immense physical pain on that Christmas Day of 1972. It was only my uncharacteristic behaviour, pushing my younger sister off my bed (we shared a bedroom), that had alerted them to the severity of my situation.

I was in a great deal of pain and just wanted to lie on my own bed. One can only wonder what might have happened if I'd been able to do that. Would I have held back long enough to have inadvertently brought about my own death?

Humans have a strong survival instinct, and I am no exception. The 'I' is my essence, my spirit, my chi, the life force that resides in me. According to psychoanalytic psychology, the ego, which operates according to the reality principle, fears death.[1] Protection of this 'I', then, takes precedence over letting others know of my pain, be it physical or emotional.

It makes sense then that my family was unaware that I was suffering from depression in 1981. I had lost weight, was withdrawn, irritable and not my usual bouncy self. Everything felt black. I had no words; they were heavy and difficult to string together. It was easier to keep going than try to explain. I was only eighteen. I didn't know that I was ill and that my illness had a name.

The human body has an amazing capacity to heal itself and mine did, in its own time. It was an agonising ten weeks, and I was very relieved to be able to put it behind me. It haunted me for a long time after. Why did it happen? I couldn't identify any triggers. People didn't talk about mental illness then: the stigma was immense. People feared being labelled crazy and being put into an asylum where unpleasant treatment practices were conducted. Unsurprisingly, I didn't talk about my depressive episode for a long time.

Two years later, a family member fell ill with the same illness, depression, and I fell into the role of caregiver. It was a long, hard stretch during which I balanced the dual roles of caring and working full-time. Fortunately, I was working in a small, quiet branch of a bank and my duties were not too onerous. Home life was a different story. My family member's depression was deeper than mine had been, and this person was unable to function. The only outside support I had was the family GP. I had no choice – I had to be strong.

Again, the illness remitted after about two months, and life returned to normal. Seeing how tired I was, my GP wrote me a medical certificate and I had two weeks off work. The relief was enormous. I could be a regular twenty-year-old again. I could go to the pub, go dancing, have a few drinks, let my hair down. It meant going to football matches (I am a Collingwood supporter) and enjoying life again. I put the challenging time behind me.

As I was emerging from this difficult period, a mutual friend with whom I played women's cricket convinced me to come and play indoor cricket, a sport that was beginning to develop a following. I hadn't been keen, but I'm glad I gave in as my now husband was part of the team. I liked him immediately and asked him out, unusual in 1983. After just six months of dating, we announced our engagement. David was living independently so we talked about living together, but we agreed that me staying at home until the wedding would be a better financial strategy.

The date was set for 17 November. Planning the wedding was exhilarating. In 1984, most people still got married in a church, and we were no exception. I lay-byed a wedding gown. There were invitations to send, a guest list to finalise, a reception venue to book. I chose bridesmaids, David chose groomsmen and we chose their dresses and suits. Colours and designs for invitations, napkins, flowers for the church pews, all of these needed our careful attention. It was an exciting time. Except that for one family member, it wasn't.

It was a different family member who became ill this time with the same illness that seemed to haunt the family – depression. I don't mind admitting that I became a little jealous when the attention began to focus on this person. I was getting married. I was the centre of attention and I loved it. But there it was again, depression, haunting me, threatening to drag me down. I couldn't let that happen. Once again, I needed to be strong, for me if for no one else. This was my time to shine, and I didn't want anyone stealing the limelight from me.

Fortunately, this family member recovered and was able to participate in the wedding when November came around. It was a joyous occasion. I felt supported and loved by my family, but it was time to leave the nest. David and I had bought a house. We moved in as soon as we returned from our honeymoon, and we set about adjusting to our new life circumstances.

Sadly, the anti-climax in the weeks following the happy event led the first family member into another episode of depression, a bad one for a person whose depression is so deep that they are unable to function and become bedridden. I felt guilty that I wasn't there to support this person and other family members. That was my role, to be the strong one, and I wasn't fulfilling it. My husband gently pointed out that I was married now, and that I was entitled to live my own life. I knew he was right, but I still felt torn. I should have been there.

It may be that my absence forced a change. I can't be certain, but it was finally decided that it was time for the family member to consult a psychiatrist. Professional help was needed. The diagnosis was 'mood swings', and a new medication prescribed. I now understand that 'mood swings' means bipolar disorder, but I didn't know that then. What was encouraging were the reports from other family members of a rapid response to this new medication. I could get on with my life again. Everything was going to be okay.

And it was for a few years, but then it wasn't. This time it was me. I've never understood why I slid into depression in 1988. I now know that I have bipolar genes in me and that bipolar has a life of its own – endogenous, arising within. I may never know the reason, and it doesn't matter now. What matters is that when I consulted the family GP complaining vaguely of not feeling like myself, he picked up on my depression and prescribed amitriptyline – a first-generation antidepressant.

First-generation antidepressants were first prescribed in the late 1950s. Tricyclics such as amitriptyline and monoamine oxidase inhibitors such as phenelzine were dominant at this time. They had serious side effects, including death should a depressed person overdose on them. Second-generation antidepressants, introduced in the late 1980s, comprise mainly selective serotonin reuptake inhibitors (for example, fluoxetine) and selective serotonin and/or norepinephrine reuptake inhibitors (for example, venlafaxine), said to be more effective with reduced toxicity. However, they have their own adverse reactions, one of which, as I have experienced, is a severe withdrawal syndrome.[2]

As with the earlier episode a few years prior, I went to work and just carried on. I didn't want to lose my job. I remained strong. Being strong has its advantages. I'm also fortunate in that my episodes of depression, while agonisingly painful, don't prevent me from functioning. Difficult, yes; impossible, no. I got through.

A year later, following a period of high stress after losing the job I'd left the bank to pursue, I found myself back in the black hole of the horrible mental illness that we call depression. Again, my GP prescribed amitriptyline and again, somehow, I managed to get through, even managing to briefly hold down a new job. For reasons not of my own doing, that job fell through, and I was fortunate to be offered another job soon after. A short time later, I became pregnant with my son and, although already on the road to recovery, this lifted me up and out of that sorry episode. I was quickly weaned off the amitriptyline and didn't look back. I was going to be a mother. There was much to be happy about.

The early years of motherhood, while challenging, were also very rewarding. Even the challenging diagnoses of my son's autism and my own secondary infertility, while eliciting powerful grief, did not lead to the illness of depression. I was focused on being the best mother I could be. It gave my life a purpose that I hadn't had before.

My old GP was no longer delivering babies, and I had moved house before Jason was born, so I opted to go local. I was fortunate to meet my current GP just as he was entering general practice. My hope was that he would never know of my earlier battles with mental illness. I was ashamed. I had taken onboard society's stigma and believed it was a weakness of character. Unfortunately, my hope was in vain.

As in 1989, a prolonged period of great stress in 1997 had

me floundering. Suffering anxiety and insomnia, I consulted my GP, seeking something to relieve the symptoms. The idea of depression hadn't entered my head, but he was alert. Recognising the months of unrelenting stress, he correctly diagnosed depression, but didn't name it. It wasn't until I filled the prescription and realised he had given me an antidepressant that I cottoned on. I hated myself. I really didn't want him to have ever seen me like this. The past was supposed to have stayed in the past. Except that it hadn't. The past and present had met and what happened next would also shape the future for many years to come.

My distrust of antidepressant medication

Treating my mood disorder

The paroxetine my GP had prescribed lifted my mood within just two weeks. Initially, the physical anxiety abated, and it was then that I recognised and named it – my old friend, depression. In this moment, for the first time, I accepted my illness.

The insomnia settled, and I was able to function properly again. My GP suggested that I stay on the paroxetine for a period of nine months, thus allowing my body to stabilise. I'd had no difficulty in weaning off the amitriptyline and thought this would be no different. Little did I know. Of course, at that point I had not dealt with what I now know

Raising a disabled son while studying is a lot to take on. In addition, my husband and I had agreed that we would have our children first and travel later. Later was now. I couldn't deny him the opportunity. Fair's fair.

Studying for my degree and diploma was stressful. Being a fast serotonin processor, a feature of bipolar disorder not known to me at the time, I found that the stress would hit around the middle of semester. I soon fell into a pattern of increasing my paroxetine dose from 20 to 30 mg midway through semester one, and again from 30 to 40 mg in semester two. Over the summers, things settled, and I was able to reduce it back from 40 to 30 mg and later to 20 mg without incident. My GP was aware, but he trusted me and chose not to intervene. It seemed no harm was being done. I believed I was treating my illness, and in a way I was, but with the wrong medication. All was okay until late 2008 when issues with the drug first reared their ugly head. As happened so many times in the years following, sleep disruption was an issue.

In the context of this narrative, the details of my lengthy battles with antidepressants are not important. It is the struggle to find a way through some agonisingly tough times that is. With that in mind, beginning in 2009, I switched drugs three times: paroxetine to escitalopram (a drug that made me suicidal), escitalopram to duloxetine and a psychiatrist whom I found to be arrogant, and finally, having found an online peer support group, back to paroxetine to stabilise. The experiences of this nine-month period provided a confronting realisation of the power of modern antidepressants. I wrote the following post on an antidepressant withdrawal forum:

> I'm scared witless. In the last few months I've gone from being a 4th-year psychology graduate, and a capable person who orchestrated moving house, to barely being able to sleep at night. I lay in bed until 11 am because I was too afraid to get up and face the day ... I really don't know how to deal with this.

I remember sitting in my bedroom, with a handful of sleeping tablets, trying to decide whether to swallow them. I think I realised that swallowing them wouldn't make things any better. It would only be a cry for help – and the medical profession would only give me more drugs.

I learned that chopping and changing these powerful drugs was not the answer. I was also learning that mainstream medicine, while capable of putting people on these drugs, was not so erudite on what to do to get us off them. This was a powerful realisation. I needed to be strong to get through this journey and free myself from the powerful grip of paroxetine, and I needed to do it without the support of the medical profession.

I had already sought help from the naturopath with whom I would forge a strong relationship for many years to come. She did not disappoint. We had many long chats about the ills of Big Pharma and the damage psychiatric medicine can do. I remained unconvinced, however, that people should never be on psychotropic drugs as I had seen too much in my formative years. This belief played out on antidepressant withdrawal forums online in the next few years as I stood firm against the extremism that seemed to prevail. Yet I wanted to believe that I didn't need this medication, that I was going to get off paroxetine and be okay. The long tapering-off process began.

Notwithstanding the paroxetine-induced weight gain that saw me balloon from 62 to 110 kg, and the lap-band surgery I had in November 2011 to counter it, my next big challenge came in 2013. I had been studying a Graduate Certificate in Loss and Grief Counselling with the aim of specialising in that field and was volunteering as a telephone counsellor at Griefline[3] (a telephone helpline), to gain practical experience. The latter was a time I found really satisfying. I was growing in the role of a counsellor and felt well-supported together with a sense of belonging.

Sadly, given night after night of battling unrelenting insomnia, I had to abandon my studies. I had done all the coursework and only needed to complete a practical assessment. It's hard to do this when sleep is not one's friend, so I gave in to the struggle and focused on my immediate health challenges. I had hoped I could pick it up later, but as time went on, I knew this wouldn't happen. I was able to continue my volunteer work with Griefline, which was good as I had something to hang on to. After the failure of IVF, I had reconstructed my sense of self and worked hard to achieve my goals and dreams. (Even now, with a completed Postgraduate Diploma in Psychology, I am unable to register as a counsellor. Sometimes life just isn't fair.)

Back to the issue at hand, my symptoms included elevated levels of cortisol, gastrointestinal issues and the insane insomnia that prevented me from sleeping more than four hours per night for a solid three-month period. This was soul-destroying, and I was desperate. At the urging of my GP, I gave in and began taking a low dose of amitriptyline just to get some sleep. I only agreed because I knew it was easy to stop at will. My distrust of psychiatric medicine was growing. But in the wee hours one sleepless night, feeling that I didn't want to be here anymore, it came into my head that 'my son needs me'. I needed to be here for him. I needed to be strong. I took the amitriptyline and held on.

Finally, my naturopath discovered the cause of my symptoms, a form of hypothyroidism called Reverse T3 Syndrome. A blood test revealed that my rT3, which prevents the uptake of free T3 at the cellular level, was 553. It should be between 170 and 450. It was a relief to know what was going on. To my horror, I discovered that mainstream medicine didn't recognise the condition and couldn't help me. I had hoped that a visit to an endocrinologist would allow me to take thyroxine or similar, thus providing rapid relief from my symptoms. This was not to be, and I was forced to rely on naturopathic remedies.

It now seemed like my body was working against me. I was taking the amitriptyline for its sedative effect, but it was a gamble. Many people find this drug very sedating. Not me, not in the past and not now. My body kept adapting, and I kept increasing the dose. My GP was happy for me to titrate up to 150 mg if needed and left it in my hands as I was going overseas on holiday. We agreed that I needed to watch out for serotonin syndrome – a potentially life-threatening condition of high-level serotonin increases caused by medications.

I only got as far as 75 mg before my heart was beating with such force that it prevented me from the very thing it was meant to help me achieve, sleep. This was tachycardia, a symptom of serotonin syndrome. Great! I was on a trip to Canada at the time. I stopped the amitriptyline and paroxetine for a few days before reinstating the paroxetine, and thankfully it settled. I had dodged a bullet, but it was a horrifying experience.

The herbal remedies began to kick in, and slowly the hypothyroidism symptoms began to settle. I had navigated my way through an incredibly challenging few months. Getting regular sleep again was heaven. I'd almost forgotten what that was like. Feeling reflective, I thought about how paroxetine was loosening its grip on me. In an online forum, I wrote:

Some subtle changes in my everyday functioning ... a deepening of my emotional responses ... whereas before I just didn't feel anything; and my spirituality is returning – along with my ability to connect with nature/music/the arts, things I was always able to do. It's like my true ability to feel is returning ...

I wanted to be off this drug. I wanted 'me' back. But as with many things in my life, things were about to take an unexpected twist.

A constellation of continuing paroxetine withdrawal symptoms had me considering switching to another antidepressant. Some people had found using another antidepressant as a bridge to getting off paroxetine a successful strategy, and another bout with insomnia saw me considering this as an option. The risk was that another drug would not cover the withdrawal from the first. While on a trip to Perth, I made my decision. I'd had enough of the constant gastrointestinal issues, and now my moods were beginning to swing. It was time to try something different. My GP supported me, and I switched to citalopram, a calming antidepressant. My naturopath also supported me, feeling that I did need to find a way to stabilise.

Unfortunately, while the new drug settled the mood swings and agitation, thus giving me relief, I had to endure three and a half years of horrific withdrawal from the paroxetine. Issues included the development of asthma, hay fever and other nasal issues, hormone imbalances mirroring menopause (despite the absence of ovaries and being on hormone replacement therapy), continuing insomnia and eventually a pattern of waves and windows. In online withdrawal forums, this phenomenon is well known and is considered characteristic of the healing process. Waves are the bad patches, windows the good ones. Over time, the waves become less frequent and eventually settle.

For me, however, the insomnia didn't settle. Not being able to approach day-to-day life with any certainty – it is very hard to function when sleep is a lottery (some nights I slept well, some I didn't) – I felt defeated. I had been using zopiclone (a hypnotic drug) intermittently, desperately trying to avoid physical dependency. But I had a husband and disabled son to care for. It wasn't all about me. I chose to stay on the zopiclone indefinitely. Reluctantly, I was now on sleeping tablets.

In a personal blog, I wrote, 'On 15 October it will mark three years since I took my last 13 mg dose of paroxetine. It is still hard to believe that ceasing that dose abruptly could have such a powerful effect on my body'. I was glad to be free of it.

Some insights I gained during this horrific period include:

I knew when my [spirit] guides were telling me that this was the right path, that it wasn't the end of the hard times. Just that I was now on the right path. I have to hold on to that. (October 2013)

It now seems clear that long-term medication was *not* right for me. I just wanted to believe that it was. I wanted to be free of the fear of clinical depression and the angst of the horrible episodes of what is lamely called 'anxiety'. I wanted to control that. (June 2015)

Changing from paroxetine to citalopram, while a useful stabilising strategy, brought its own issues. Within a few months, my naturopath discovered that my melatonin levels were low. I commenced supplementation in mid-2014, increasing it in 2016 and twice in 2017. The drug merry-go-round never seemed to stop. I had felt good in 2017 – no sleep issues, and stable moods regardless of life stressors. If not for the melatonin issue, I would have happily stayed on the citalopram.

I'd also had to deal with my son being diagnosed with bipolar disorder in August 2014. I was now a mental health caregiver as well as a disability caregiver. My struggles with antidepressants had included some heated debate in online forums around whether psychotropic medications were an option for anyone; a stance I had defended resolutely. Even though I had wanted to take my son off fluoxetine, I found myself doing a 180-degree turn following his diagnosis of bipolar. I was apprehensive about him being on long-term medication but eventually decided that quality of life was the most important factor. He had been having hypomanic episodes interspersed with mixed depressive episodes, in which features of mania and depression giving rise to agitated depression are present at the same time. There were only a few weeks between each of these. I couldn't let him live life like that, not when there was something I could do to make life better for him.

I decided that long-term medication was right for him, but not for me. The latter belief saw me determined to get off citalopram, despite some very challenging times over the next few years. I did not trust antidepressants and resolved that, once off them, I would never take them again.

Hiatus in my struggle and a revelation

During 2016 and 2017, enjoying a period of stability in my antidepressant journey, I stayed on the citalopram and zopiclone while increasing the melatonin from 6 to 13 mg. I knew I was going to have to taper off the antidepressant so I could end my body's reliance on melatonin. Continuing to increase the dose was not a healthy option.

While enjoying that period of stability, another issue arose which led to an unexpected breakthrough in terms of repressed memories. A violent attack on a footballer at my son's club during a game, which rendered him unconscious and in need of an ambulance, had me writing in two voices. One was about what I had witnessed on the football field, the other was me as a young girl. When I was a young child, I always drew my people with no arms. My artwork is very average, and my people were little more than stick figures, but they never had arms. As I was writing, my jaw dropped, and I had a flash of insight. In the horrific violent attack on me in the past life about which I wrote in my prequel, I had curled up in a foetal ball on my bed with my arms raised to shield my head. My father was stronger than me, and my arms couldn't protect me from the beating that led to my death.

My arms couldn't protect me.

I still have a childhood painting that my mother kept, something about it winning first prize in a competition because it demonstrated 'good balance'. In that painting, named *Me and my cat*, (I have always been a cat lover), my portrait of myself is an interesting study. The body, depicted without arms, is painted in black, while the head is pink with a smiling face. Could it be that I was expressing a dark past where arms were useless, while being happy in the present? That is certainly my interpretation.

Witnessing that violent attack in which the victim was hurt, something I'd never witnessed before in this life, triggered a memory from my past life. In that life, I wasn't strong enough. In this life, I have issues with always being the strong one. One was physical, the other more about determination, but the parallels are intriguing. I pulled a book out of my bookshelf about past-life experiences, and it encouraged me to change the outcome in my mind, to take back the power. Instead of cowering in a foetal ball on my bed, I imagined myself standing in front of my father and pushing him so hard that he fell out of the window and down from the second storey to the ground below. He would not hurt me again. It was a liberating experience. Now I needed to liberate myself from psychiatric drugs, beginning with the citalopram. Time to be strong again.

CHAPTER 2

When mental health issues and antidepressant withdrawal collide

I was apprehensive about tapering off the citalopram. I really didn't want to go through withdrawal issues a second time. The stability had been a relief, but I couldn't keep increasing the dose of melatonin. Despite my fears, I began tapering off in February 2018 and had successfully dropped from 20 mg to 16 mg by August. Struggling with the withdrawal of the latter dose, I hesitated, up-dosed briefly and sought advice from an online forum. Reassured, I went back to 16 mg and stayed there for a few months. At that point, following several months of practising yoga, it came to me:

I am safe in the universe.

What happened before is not going to happen again.

Spiritually, I believed that my higher self was communicating with me, and in the silence, my soul listened. Fortified by this, I continued tapering off in 2019, finishing the year on 11 mg. It was going well.

Unfortunately, other parts of my life were not. We had a marriage breakdown in October 2018, and by the early months of 2019, reconciliation had not been achieved. Not liking the person I was becoming, I changed my behaviour by reining in my emotional outbursts and cynicism. Complicating things was the development of a significant issue with our investment property, a commercial office suite. Our neighbours in the office building wanted to separate the two lots, built as one joint tenancy, and without warning, we were hit with a large quote. We declined and when the current tenants vacated, put the property on the market. To our horror, we discovered that it was worth a lot less than we had paid for it. At best, we could pay off our debts. Our stress levels were high.

Then my husband had a serious car accident that was not of his making. He was physically unharmed but could have killed others or been killed. Some say he should have bought a lottery ticket. I couldn't deal with it and dissociated. I was angry that, as I was trying to decide whether to end the marriage or not, my choice could have been taken from me. I didn't feel any empathy towards him. There were echoes of a previous trauma here. Choice was important to me. Three weeks later, our disabled son was in a car accident. Again, he was unharmed, but the possibility that I could have lost both of them haunted me for some time.

Writing feverishly (writing has always been my release), I sought to understand the deeper meaning and therefore the motivation behind my struggles. As I listened to the messages coming from the deepest recesses of my very existence, a profound revelation occurred. In the IVF years, I had felt helpless and unable to engineer a positive outcome. David's car accident could have resulted in a sense of helplessness together with a negative outcome. That it didn't meant that I could influence the future, if not the past. I had not been heard when my arms couldn't protect or save me. I had not spoken up when I had been in immense pain due to acute appendicitis and had almost died. My pain due to the failure of IVF had been silent, with many people not understanding the trauma of the complete helplessness. I made a resolution. I would never *not* be heard again.

Just in case I didn't have enough to deal with, every household maintenance issue that could have gone wrong that year did. The financial uncertainty of the property, the drain on our current finances, the unresolved marital situation and the dual car accidents saw me on high doses of serotonin-boosting tablets and adrenal-calming naturopathic supplements. My feeling was that without these, I would have suffered depression that year. As it was, my unprecedented call to Lifeline in November resulted in a visit to the local Emergency Department (ED) and a diagnosis of acute stress reaction, a disorder similar to post-traumatic stress disorder but transient. I had felt compelled to self-harm, something I'd not felt or done before, and I knew I had to fight it.

Since self-harm had never been part of my earlier mental health struggles, I will always wonder about the considerable amounts of naturopathic medicine I was consuming and if this had somehow changed how I broke down under stress. Being deficient in melatonin had me wanting to binge eat. Then again, I had experienced trauma. I will never know. I do know that I got through it all without increasing or adding psychotropic medication, convincing myself that it could be done, so after some time out to recover from the trauma, and some counselling, I resumed tapering off the citalopram.

While in recovery, the universe opened an opportunity and presented me an offer I couldn't refuse. Would I be interested in going on a cruise to New Zealand with a girlfriend's sister at short notice? With the financial uncertainty we'd been experiencing, causing me to release the money I had saved on behalf of my son to use as needed, I figured that I might as well. I didn't know what the future held. Our marriage was still strained. Additionally, I'd never left David and Jason to go away before. I felt the music of the universe reverberating through me and decided to join in. I went to New Zealand.

Early in 2020, I rejoined my husband and son for the less luxurious but fun cruise we had booked destined for Adelaide. I had come back from the first cruise having resolved to sort out my marriage and to begin the push for Jason to go into supported housing. Best laid plans … What I got was a Covid pandemic and a long lockdown that left me feeling helpless and angry.

If I had never thought I would experience a pandemic, I certainly never dreamed that Melbourne would be put into a harsh lockdown and kept that way for four long months. It was the world's longest lockdown, beginning on 9 July and ending at midnight on 26 October. I had always loved Melbourne, and I was left with a desire to understand why I felt so attached to my home city. Melbourne, as I later discovered, is very much the city of my ancestors, right back to the gold rush period of the 1850s. I am a Melburnian of five generations. The loss of freedom shook me to my core. I never thought it would happen here. I watched in horror the over-exertion of force used to enforce the very restrictive rules of the lockdown, wondering what had happened to the city I had always loved, the city once known as Marvellous Melbourne. Worse, I didn't like the style of government I was seeing or the results of the hotel quarantine enquiry in which all the key players seemed to have developed amnesia. What had happened to democracy? To freedom? I felt trapped. My home city was no longer the safe and free place I had always known. I was deeply shaken. But this is politics, and I can't control that. Writing letters to politicians, while unproductive, empowered me, though, and I remained resolute. I would get through this.

At the height of the lockdown, the harsh reality of no longer being physically able to keep up with my disabled son confronted me. I was fifty-nine years old, and I am only one person. When allowed, I took him to a park for afternoon tea and some exercise. We had no supports for a week and a half. His day program had been forced to close for the school holidays, and they were not allowed to run holiday programs. I felt disconnected from society, old and alone.

Despite the frustration and helplessness, my mood had been good, and I had found the slower pace of life during the lockdown refreshing. Even hiring a lawyer and searching fruitlessly for resolution to the property deadlock – a potential sale having fallen through, we had agreed to the subdivision but could not agree on a quote or a builder – did not overwhelm me. I was able to reduce the naturopathic supplements to just two serotonin-boosting tablets per day and the citalopram from 11 mg to 7.4 mg.

Covid had been a shock. I reasoned that 2021 would be better, that there would be no more lockdowns. I was wrong. I certainly didn't expect another long lockdown, a near repeat of the one of 2020, albeit a few weeks shorter. I also believed that I would never suffer depression again and that I could manage my mental health issues with naturopathic remedies and things like yoga and meditation. I was wrong about that, too.

My first citalopram dose reduction of 2021 triggered a response reminiscent of the paroxetine withdrawal crash that had unleashed a horrific thyroid issue. Knowing this was a critical dose range in terms of its effect on receptors in the brain (something I learned during my years in online antidepressant withdrawal communities), I decided to stay on 7 mg until things settled. There was no rush. I had already been on this journey for twelve years.

Meanwhile, I was having what I now call 're-entry anxiety' as I struggled to adjust to life after the long Covid lockdown of 2020 and the diagnosis of osteoarthritis in my lower back. Even more unsettling was the sale of our investment property in March. We had accepted an offer that was significantly lower than that of a year ago, further agreeing to reduce the price to allow for the new owners to pay for the subdivision, as we just wanted out. Settlement, while a relief, was unsettling in many ways. It had been a two-year saga and a source of marital discord and ongoing financial uncertainty. I needed time to settle my mind.

If I'd been able, I would have liked to have had time to process the enormity of it all now that the two-year saga had finally come to an end. We had suffered a large capital loss, spent thousands on legal fees and really, if not for the savings from my son's unspent pension over many years, could have been in real financial trouble, liquidity-wise at least. We had plenty of equity in our home so thankfully we were not at risk of becoming homeless. But time waits for no one, and I didn't have time to settle.

Indeed, being settled would not be part of my life for many months to come. Amid the tsunami that followed, I received the message, 'you are strong', on more than one occasion, somehow minimising, I felt, my personal struggles and invalidating my need for support when times get tough. I might be strong, but I am not indestructible.

Dad phoned one morning in April, just three weeks after settlement on the property went through, leaving a message on my voicemail. Mum had become unwell, and he didn't know what to do. He didn't call my younger sister because 'she has her own issues'. I felt that my struggles, including a son with multiple disabilities, were not being recognised. I didn't take the call. He said he was going to call my brother next, so I left it and went back to bed. I set a boundary when I later conversed with my brother: I was already a caregiver so I couldn't take on that role with Mum and Dad, as much as I love them. But I can't just turn off caring.

Battling insomnia, nervous system hyperarousal and with a sense of drowning, I soon found myself contemplating taking an overdose. I knew I couldn't let that happen, so I called a mental health triage phone number on 3 May. I was referred to the Casey Crisis Assessment and Treatment Team (CATT) and received a combination of face-to-face and telehealth support for the next week.

Two things about that week disturbed me. When the psychiatrist diagnosed depression, he wasn't amenable to my struggle with antidepressants, despite a lengthy explanation of what they had done to me. He wanted me to increase the dose of citalopram. I was adamant that I wasn't going to. Nothing else was suggested. Were antidepressants his only method of treating my illness? I had outlined the family history of bipolar disorder: was a mood stabiliser not an option? I felt that he wasn't listening and left that appointment dissatisfied.

A few days later, knowing that I was seeing my GP, the team discharged me with a resounding 'this is a testament to how strong you are' message. I didn't feel strong at all, yet I remained silent. Despite my vow to never not be heard again, my unconscious need to protect my 'id' from its vulnerabilities prevented me from telling the team that I wasn't ready or that I didn't feel good. In fact, I felt very let down.

The diagnosis of depression had come as a shock. It had been an incredibly challenging year in 2019, but I had got through it without an appearance from my old friend. Using a combination of psychiatric drugs and naturopathic medicine, together with exercise and stints of counselling/psychology support, I had managed to keep it at bay for twenty-four years. My coping skills were better, and I really wanted to believe that, once off the drugs, I would not suffer depression again. I could not have been more wrong.

What was different now in 2021? The deep frustration of the long lockdown of 2020, the re-entry anxiety and adjustment difficulties, alongside the financial uncertainty and helplessness of what had happened with our investment property, and normal stress related to doing administration work for my son's football club were simply too much. Stress overload – this was what caused my depression.

There may have been an element of citalopram withdrawal here too. Past experience and several years of inhabiting antidepressant withdrawal forums online have taught me that these drugs have their greatest effect in low doses, something to do with serotonin transport occupancy in the receiving neuron. Apparently, this falls off a cliff at a certain dose range – 11–14 mg with paroxetine and apparently around 7 mg with citalopram.

Having been discharged by the Casey CATT, I consulted with my GP. I had made a long appointment (thirty minutes) and taken my husband with me for support. I don't normally take my husband with me, and I felt that this should have been a red flag. This appointment was interrupted at least three times, and I was pushed through in fifteen minutes. Again, I felt very let down. I was vulnerable and felt that I wasn't important enough to receive the level of care afforded to others. I don't blame my GP as he did his best. To be fair, he has since pointed out that I have a higher coping capacity than most and that people often think that people like me will always be okay. Nonetheless, I felt that the level of my pain wasn't being taken seriously enough and was very disappointed.

Fortunately, naturopathic remedies saved the day, and I went off to battle the numerous issues with Mum's hospital admission and Dad's need for support in the home. I let my brother lead, choosing a supportive role, and did what I could among more Covid lockdowns and the uncertainty of the future of my elderly parents. After numerous telehealth consultations between my mum's treating doctors, my brother and myself, Mum appeared to be recovering. On 5

August, I took her home. That afternoon, I took my son to have his first Covid vaccine and Melbourne went back into lockdown. Sadly, Mum's time at home was short-lived. She was readmitted to hospital just four days later and never went home again. Covid restrictions meant that I couldn't visit her. It was heart-wrenching.

Meanwhile, knowing that we were caregivers, my brother and I were allowed to visit Dad regularly, my brother facilitating a range of supports while battling the aged care system. Dad put on a brave face, but he was struggling. I knew Mum and Dad would both go into residential aged care; my brother needed a little longer to realise this and we both wanted to give them the dignity of making their own decision.

Visiting Dad every weekend was tiring. Compounding the physical stress were the powerful waves of grief I was experiencing. Grief is adaptive, and I had yet to adapt to the rapidly changing circumstances of my parents' lives. I wrote copious words, my profound emotions spilling onto the pages of reams of paper. Another coping strategy was to retreat into a time when my family of origin was intact – my childhood – and I thoroughly enjoyed watching every episode of reruns of *Star Trek: The Original* on Foxtel while reliving fond memories. I felt comforted and safe.

Grief can be negotiated without mental health issues, but it can also lead to depression. Part of my anticipatory grief had been not wanting to lose my mother. Going into care would mean she was a lot closer to the end. If she was going to die, I wanted to go with her. *We could go together*, I thought. With such powerful emotions coursing through me, and given the stresses I had already endured, it was not surprising then that my old friend, depression, returned for another visit.

This time, I quickly became suicidal. I had not felt this way since my first episode of depression forty years earlier. It was now September, just five months since I had contacted mental health services seeking help in fighting a desire to take an overdose. This time, however, there was not going to be any help-seeking. I was going to take my own life, and I began making plans. I wrote down what songs I wanted played at my funeral and how I wanted to be remembered and started penning a 'sorry' letter for all those I was leaving behind. I felt disbelief that I was making these plans but had no doubts about my intent. I wanted to die.

There was one immediate obstacle I had to overcome first. I was going to take an overdose of zopiclone, but my supply was low. I needed a prescription, so I scheduled an appointment with my GP. Meanwhile, I had given a sample of my hair to my naturopath who sent it off for a hair mineral analysis. I was curious and wondered what it would reveal. What could she do for me? I needed to wait a couple of weeks. I was wavering. Later, I pondered my decision to hold on until

I received the results of that hair analysis. What was I waiting for? Several months later, I worked it out: *I wanted someone to care enough to want to save me.* This was another powerful revelation and I felt that it related to how I had died in my previous life.

The spiritual can also be very powerful, and what happened next was no exception. I had a dream. I was lost in the woods. Not knowing how I got there, I became a passenger in a car, and Mum was driving. I said, 'Oh, you're here'. She said, 'Yes, I am', straightened the wheel and put the car back on the road. When I woke up, I felt Mum's energy next to me – I am clairsentient – and she made it known that it was her and that she 'wasn't done yet'. I don't know how I knew that it was Mum, but I did. My mother was my rescuer. During her medical treatment, her psychic energy had reached out to me. I was incredulous. How could this happen? *Mum had cared enough to want to save me.*

Adding to this profound experience, the next morning I had what I understand to be a lucid dream. It felt ethereal. I was aware as I was dreaming that I could influence the outcome. I saw a light switch. I was deciding: if I pressed 'on', I was choosing life; 'off' was death. My hand hovered. I wanted death, but the visitation from Mum had strengthened me. Knowing it would be hard, I chose life and the dream ended.

Naturopathically, the hair mineral analysis revealed several health issues, including low magnesium (implicated in depression), malabsorption and an under-functioning parasympathetic nervous system affecting my ability to enjoy refreshing rest and to properly digest food. My naturopath said that many people's nervous systems had been adversely affected by the Covid lockdowns. In my case, the frustration had bubbled along internally, affecting my overall health. I struggled to take all the remedies she prescribed but thought it was worth a try. If I was going to live, I needed to regain my physical health and my mood.

Within about three weeks, I felt brighter and refocused my efforts on Mum and Dad. Mum moved from hospital to transitional care in late October and Melbourne came out of lockdown. She had admitted to me that she needed to go into aged care, and my brother was able to facilitate her admission into an appropriate place a few days before Christmas. This was a relief as her mood had become low again and it was either there or readmission to hospital. The latter would have been a backward step and we were keen to avoid it.

Dad needed a higher level of support as well. He was forgetting to take his medicines. When VicRoads cancelled his driver's licence following his diagnosis of Alzheimer's, it wasn't difficult to convince him to follow Mum into care. I felt relieved. After more than sixty years of marriage, Mum and Dad were now in the same place. My brother and I had worked tirelessly to keep them together. We had achieved our objective. It was a good feeling.

CHAPTER 3

I am only one person

It was now mid-January 2022, and I was tired. My battles with depression and grief during previous months had taken their toll. I was now a sandwich caregiver, caring for my ageing parents and my disabled son at the same time. There was work to be done, though, and my brother and I set about clearing out Mum and Dad's house and preparing for it to be put on the market. An end was in sight. I could do this. I could keep going.

Famous last words!

A hurtful comment by someone about my son by a long-term acquaintance at an Australia Day gathering of friends hit a nerve. I was already exhausted from being a caregiver for multiple people: Mum with an illness requiring a lot of treatment and care, Dad with Alzheimer's, Jason with autism, intellectual disability, ADHD, and bipolar disorder II and the concomitant demands of negotiating NDIS supports. I didn't need this.

Saying, 'Let's face it, he's different, isn't he?' in a tentative tone of voice hit me like a slap across the face. Really? Had she just noticed this? What have I been doing for the past thirty-two years? She's known Jason since he was born, and I've never hidden my struggles or his disabilities. There were other comments that day too, comments that hit out at my role as a caregiver; it seems that she thought they were jokes. Some people have a strange sense of humour. I was stunned, too stunned to do more than limply point out that we've known that Jason was disabled since 1994 – twenty-eight years ago. It's not exactly hurtful to talk about the reality of our everyday lives, not after all these years. Quite the opposite, actually. What was hurtful was not being able to see beyond the barrier of disability and see my son as a human being, with his wicked sense of humour, infectious laugh, beautiful smile and gentle nature.

Additionally, I felt that my husband didn't listen to me when I tried to talk to him about it. The acquaintance wanted to gatecrash a boys' lunch that he had booked at the local RSL. She had invited me to join her, but I had declined. I don't believe in that sort of behaviour, not at our time of life, and certainly not when there are Covid density limits in public places. David said it wasn't important to him and kept pushing my concerns aside. Not being heard is a theme in my life, and I was not going to let it keep happening. My needs are as important as anyone else's, especially when I have been hurt so deeply. I needed him to be on my side. It was important.

This issue ultimately caused a major schism between my husband and me. There had been progress in our marital discord over the past three years, and I had decided to stay in the marriage, but I was in pain, and I needed to be heard. Echoes of the past ran deep.

Adding to my pain, the cat that had come to live with us when Mum and Dad went into care was diagnosed with cancer, and in March, sadly, had to be put to sleep. I was gutted. Her female energy had been a bright star in the continuing gloom of hard work and striving without end. The good news was that my parents' house had been sold.

Somehow, I got caught in a slipstream and found myself falling into the role of being Mum's caregiver. Each visit had me leaving with a list of things to get for her. Driving home one day, I wondered if this was ever going to end. I was already Jason's primary caregiver and was looking forward to a time when he would be in supported accommodation, though I had no idea when that would be. The last thing I needed was more caring duties. Things were starting to feel heavy.

My mood dropped again, and in late April I noticed that

I felt 'wrong'. I couldn't identify why. In my therapeutic writing, I noted a persistent and pervasive feeling of sadness. Grief was certainly part of the picture, but I didn't think it had morphed into depression. My emotions didn't seem to be functioning normally. I felt agitated and just not right. Was I just worn out, I asked myself. Probably, I thought. I am only one person after all. Things felt heavy, and suicidal thoughts crept in. Naturopathic remedies helped, and I pushed the thoughts away.

My state of mind

I had a sense of my thoughts closing in on me. It was like the world in which I sought to function was getting smaller. It seemed that I was operating solely in a world of caregiving, but no one was caring for me. Battling to hold on, I started rationalising. I just needed a holiday, I told myself. I booked a cruise for December. I could keep going until then, I told myself.

In addition, my beliefs were becoming distorted. Being to some degree clairsentient, I once felt that I would only live to be sixty-one. In hindsight, if indeed I did pick up on some sort of energy, it was about a girlfriend who, as it turned out, passed away at the age of sixty-one. I told myself that I was only eighteen months away. No matter how hard things were now, an end was in sight. I would soon be sixty-one, and there would be no more suffering. My mind was searching for an out.

Nonetheless, having grown accustomed to supporting my parents, I endeavoured to visit their nursing home fortnightly. Not allowing myself the time I needed for me, I put their needs first, as I had been doing for twelve months. I needed to stay strong and keep going. My days were mostly about doing things for others. There was little time to play. I wondered how long this was going to go on. I was miserable.

Meanwhile, preparing for my son to eventually go into supported housing meant speech therapy appointments, occupational therapy at home and in-home caregiver support shifts twice weekly. Added to this was National Disability Insurance Scheme (NDIS) paperwork and ongoing planning for various activities such as holiday programs. In early May, I expressed fatigue to the speech therapist, wondering whether the NDIA (the NDIS agency) would continue funding this therapy for much longer. We had been doing it for about three years. She encouraged me to keep going but recommended a break if needed. Talking to her made me feel better so I kept going. A similar conversation came up with the occupational therapist who offered to look for things that might help. I just wanted it all to go away.

Jason's housing application was submitted to the NDIA in July 2021, the initial response being that an outcome would be known in six to eight weeks. Several prompts to my local area coordinator since then had not borne fruit and I now had my support coordinator escalating things. Shortly before my exhaustion took control of me, an official complaint was lodged with the NDIA. As if that wasn't enough, I received a letter telling me they were going to roll over Jason's current plan. I wanted to scream, *No! I need this housing thing sorted asap!*

Things were feeling very heavy, and I was not in control of my life. A pervasive feeling of sadness persisted. I didn't know what to do to regain control. In a strange way, my choice of words in my writing reflected a reality that I didn't yet understand.

> I'm tired, frustrated, fed up, burnt out
> I'm tired of looking after everyone else (24 April 2022)

My thoughts closed in even more. The suicidal ideation refused to go away. The weight of responsibility felt heavy with no prospect of my load being lightened any time soon. I had never felt like this before.

Suicide attempt

There was a trigger. Unlike a few months earlier, I had not meant to give in to the suicidal ideation. Sub-consciously, given the earlier messaging about not needing the same support as others, I was probably just trying to be strong.

Until something snapped.

Still in the caregiver slipstream, I allowed my parents' nursing home to play me. Mum needed to attend an appointment, and someone needed to go with her, they told me. They were aware of my son and my role as his caregiver and should not have phoned me, but my brother was unavailable, they said. (My sister lives in regional Victoria and was not available either.) A couple of phone calls later, I agreed. It would be 'girl time', I told myself, just Mum and me enjoying each other's company which I actually thought would be good. I should have said no.

The signs of caregiver burnout were already there – fatigue, decreased appetite and intermittent insomnia. I was anxious, persistently felt sad and hopeless and lacked motivation. I just tried to get through each day – and I didn't even know what I enjoyed doing anymore, it had been so long. One description of caregiver burnout speaks of 'being overwhelmed and physically, emotionally and mentally exhausted from the stress and burden of caring for their loved one'.[4] In my case, it was multiple people and caring duties. Something had to give.

On the night of 23 May 2022, I went to bed, planning to attend a University of the Third Age (U3A) group the next morning. The idea of taking an overdose had not entered my head. I fell asleep around midnight but woke at 2 am. After tossing, turning, going to the toilet and looking at my clock-radio repeatedly, I was defeated. It was 5:45 am. I went to the kitchen with the intention of taking another two zopiclone. I had taken two at bedtime, as I had been doing for the past six years. It didn't occur to me that I needed to get up at 7:30 am to assist in getting my son ready for his bus pick-up. I guess I hoped I would get at least another hour's sleep before then. I really couldn't face getting through a day on only two hours sleep, not after that horrific three-month stretch in 2013 of barely four hours of sleep per night. I was desperate. Another couple of hours of sleep would make the day bearable.

Or so I thought.

The analogue clock in the kitchen displayed the time. I moved to the cupboard above the cooktop and pulled out the box of zopiclone. I pulled out a blister strip and pressed out two tablets. The thought came into my head, *Bugger it, take them all*, and I took two handfuls, swallowing each handful with water. I think I took twenty-two tablets in all. As I was doing it, I had a strange sense of observing my actions without actively participating in them. 'I' was not in control, but I had taken an overdose.

I don't recall thinking, *I'm going to kill myself.* This may be why I dissociated, because what I was doing was too threatening to my 'self', my 'id'. I just did it and, in a daze, went back to bed. I was going to sleep. That much was certain.

My next memory is vague. It was about 8 am, and my son was about to leave for his day program. I remember him moving through the front door. David must have helped him to get ready. After that, I slept until 4 pm. Disappointed that I had woken up, I got up and headed back to the kitchen to take more pills. David had been out for most of the day and didn't realise what had happened until he caught me. I had taken four or six when he bumped me aside, causing me to hit my head against the side of the cupboard. While I stood there rubbing my head, he phoned Poisons Information. They advised him that the zopiclone may cause breathing difficulties and that I should go to the ED. Hubby told me to pack a bag, and I followed along like a lost lamb.

On the way to the hospital, he asked me if I knew where I was going. I told him that I was going 'home'. In the initial attempt at 5:45 am, I hadn't consciously decided to take my own life so I had dissociated and observed myself doing it. That afternoon, I consciously tried to finish the job. I didn't want to be here. I wanted to die.

As a result of my acute appendicitis on Christmas Day 1972, I had nearly died and had had a near-death experience. I'd had a strong sense that I was going 'home'. I don't know where 'home' was, but it was better than living in the present day. This is what I was referring to. I was going to die, and my energy was returning to where it had come from. I was looking forward to it. I wanted to go.

> I wanted to take them all
> Couldn't say exactly why
> I just wanted to finish the packet
> And if I died, I died, and I'd be free (25 May 2022)

How had things become so bad so quickly? To be honest, I'm not really sure. I do know that I didn't feel in control of my life, a symptom I now know of caregiver burnout. When I wrote about feeling 'wrong' in late April, I couldn't identify what that meant. Not surprising – I'd never suffered burnout before. I didn't know what it felt like.

I was aware there were symptoms of depression, but it didn't feel like depression. Since I didn't know what was wrong, I didn't realise that I needed help. Surely asking for help would have been better than pushing the suicidal thoughts away, or, since I'd been suicidal a few months earlier and been able to overcome it, did I think that I could do it again? If so, my expectations of myself were impossibly high. This is not unusual for me. The façade of being strong is a shield to protect my core belief of always having to fight for my survival alone.

Again, I didn't tell people that I needed help. Not physical, as I keep reasonably fit and work with a naturopath on my physical health, but no one knew that I was in such powerful mental and emotional pain.

A suicide attempt is serious, so upon my arrival at the Frankston Hospital ED, I was quickly placed at the head of a long queue. A short time later, I was escorted to a safe room, devoid of anything with which I could hurt myself and left to sleep off the effects of my overdose. There was a soft bench in there where I slept on and off, wearing my pyjamas and using my dressing gown as a pillow. I managed to text my brother at some point to let him know that I was unable to take Mum to her appointment. I was not very proud of myself for letting them down, yet I felt a strange sense of relief.

Sometime the next morning, I was moved to a cubicle and received visits from a mental health clinician and a social worker. I told them I was full of remorse for taking the overdose, but I don't think I was. I think I just told them what they needed to hear. I'm not even sure I knew what I was feeling. I was numb yet ashamed of what I'd done. They both said I was experiencing caregiver burnout which explained why I'd felt 'wrong'. I accepted mental health support and spoke to the social worker about Jason and the NDIA's lack of response in terms of the housing application that had been submitted in July 2021. The social worker said she would speak to Jason's support coordinators and advocate for the housing application on my behalf.

After some breakfast, I was discharged from hospital. It was now mid-morning on Wednesday 25 May. Still in the grip of the zopiclone overdose and feeling emotionally numb, I didn't do much on that day. I felt strange. I'd never been here before. What does one do after a suicide attempt? I was able to do some paperwork and cobble some dinner together.

On Thursday, still in a daze, I took my car in for a service. While filling in time at home, I received a phone call from the Casey CATT and accepted an appointment at Casey Hospital for the following morning. I hoped I wouldn't be seeing the same psychiatrist I had seen a year earlier. I was *not* going to take antidepressants and did not want to be told that I needed to. I was, however, receptive to the idea of a mood stabiliser as my son's psychiatrist had said something to me a few years ago that was floating around in my mind – I have bipolar genes in me.

In the haze of what I had done, something had changed. I was now able to express this:

> I've been feeling a bit like a Shirley Valentine
> > Really needing a holiday
> > I think I've gone beyond that now
> > I think I'm overwrought and feeling resentment
> > When I was studying, I worked really hard

> But I loved what I was doing
> I don't love what I'm doing anymore
> I don't love working so hard all the time
> I don't want to give out so much of <u>me</u> to others
> All the time
> I just want my time to be my own (26 May 2022)

Later that afternoon, while engaged in a speech therapy session with my son via telehealth, I received a phone call from my NDIS support coordinators. Having heard the news, and following contact with the social worker I had met in hospital, the NDIA had finally approved Jason's application for supported housing. I didn't know what to feel. This was great news, I knew that, but I was still numb and ashamed of my actions. It did put a smile on my face, though.

On Friday morning, recognising the rooms of the Casey CATT from a year earlier, I sat in the waiting room, wondering if I was wasting my time. The dissatisfaction from my last visit there played on my mind, so I was relieved to be called in by two women. The discussion was fruitful, and this time I felt heard. They had found an opening for me at a Monash Health clinic in Dandenong with a psychologist as early as Monday. The clinic also had a psychiatrist whom I could access upon request. It seemed a reasonable course of action, although I still felt numb. It was also recommended that I obtain a mental health plan from my GP to enable longer-term support than Monash Health could provide. Recovery was possible, but I needed help to move beyond the present. My thoughts, however, did not advance beyond this Monday appointment.

Reflections of a suicidal crisis

Before recounting my journey of recovery, I want to take the time to ponder the reasons for attempting suicide eight months after the initial suicidal crisis had passed. I believe I was closer to ending my life in September 2021 than I was when I took the overdose.

I have written elsewhere about the encounter with Mum's metaphysical energy on 17 September – the dream in which she rescued me from the woods, put me in a car and drove back on the road. One could call it the road of life. At that time, I was not only clinically depressed, I was also 'spiritually tired – and ready to go', as I identified in my writing a few days later. In the next few days, I wrote, 'I don't feel so desperate now' and that 'I no longer feel so desperately in pain'. Mum's intervention had saved me. The crisis had passed.

That the crisis had passed was reflected in the following, written after my lucid dream about the light switch that represented the choice I was making – life or death.

My hand hovered
   I was making a choice
   The lower button was the easier path
   It's the one I wanted to press
   But as I hovered, I felt encouraged, guided
   Almost like my hand made the 'right' decision
   Even though I wanted to take the easier path
   But I didn't
   I pressed the upper button (21 September 2021)

Before Mum's intervention, my plan had been to obtain my script for zopiclone, thus giving me the means to take an overdose. I now had the zopiclone. However, after the intervention I had chosen life, though I knew it was the harder way, and I didn't take the pills.

In May 2022, despite having suicidal thoughts, I was not clinically depressed and was keen on finding light at the end of the tunnel. Any light I thought I saw, however, appeared to be a train coming the other way, and I was stuck in the tunnel, unable to find my way through and out to the other side.

Taking an overdose was an idea I'd first had in May 2021, and I was ready to embrace it. In May 2022, it was an impulsive act and, though I did want to die, it was more likely a cry for help. I say that because I readily accepted mental health support rather than looking for another method of dying by my own hand.

So, despite the May 2022 attempt, the real crisis had been in September 2021, when I was 'spiritually tired – and ready to go'. The deeper need for 'someone to care enough to want to save me' had been met.

My mother in my past life had not been able to stand up to my violent father, and I had died by his hand. My mother in this life did care, despite undergoing her own medical treatment at the time. It was a profound experience, and it literally saved my life. A mother's love that seemingly transcends physical existence – is there any force more powerful?

CHAPTER 4

Recovery from suicidality

On Monday 30 May, still feeling numb, I arrived at my psychology appointment with Monash Health in Dandenong. I found the psychologist, G, very easy to talk to and was pleasantly surprised that she allowed our discussion to continue for nearly two hours. It was lunchtime and I was hungry, but I felt like I could have talked for hours. I walked away feeling a bit lighter.

Themes explored in this session included how long I'd been a caregiver, not just since Jason was born, but at times growing up as well. It was now time to explore how to maintain a relationship with Mum and Dad without it being too much of a burden. It was important to establish a boundary and to learn how to be 'I' again and do what I want, instead of always looking after everyone else. This would require change. The 'well' concept was considered: if we draw from the well too often, it runs dry. My well needed to be replenished.

On 2 June, following up on what the women at Casey CATT had recommended, I presented myself to my GP looking for a mental health plan. When he discovered that I had taken an overdose, he said, 'That's not like you.' His comment resonated. He had recognised the level of my pain. It meant a lot to me. I let him know that I'd waited until I could see him because I didn't want to talk to anyone else. I've known him a long time and trust him.

I had made a long appointment (thirty minutes), so I took the time to explain a bit about the level of care my brother and I had been providing to our parents over the past twelve months and how hard it had all been. Still feeling numb, I said that everything had just felt so heavy. My GP pointed out that those circumstances were unlikely to happen again and, in so doing, simultaneously validated my struggles and gave me hope for the future. I am very lucky to have him. Months later, I discovered that I had visited either Mum or Dad twenty-eight times in 2021 alone. Little wonder that I had burnt out.

I also needed a script for zopiclone, the sleeping tablet. In taking the overdose, I had, of course, depleted my supply. I knew I was going to have to stop taking them, but I was afraid of the withdrawal. My struggles with antidepressants haunted me. I really didn't want to go through that again. I had to promise to give the tablets to my husband to dispense before my GP would give me the script. A good doctor was always going to be reluctant to give me the means to overdose again, and I have a good one.

On 6 June, I tested positive for Covid and had to remain in isolation for seven days. This meant that I had to reschedule my planned session with the psychologist in Dandenong. G called to arrange a day and time to meet again and to make sure I was okay. I indicated that I was keen to see a psychiatrist, that my GP also wanted this for me, and that I needed to do it soon before the script for zopiclone ran out. A spot was available on 16 June, which I accepted. I was to see her on 14 June as well. I felt that the psychiatrist appointment was a step in the right direction.

Still in Covid isolation, I converted my next GP appointment on 10 June from face-to-face to telehealth. He wanted another long appointment so he could properly do my mental health plan. Later, when I looked at the plan, he had put nothing on it at all. It was a clever ploy. He simply wanted me to keep talking to him. His reason for doing so was vindicated when I admitted that I'd had thoughts of taking another overdose. No doubt he was relieved when I said that these had gone now. My mood was also brighter as I was relieved I was getting the help I needed. Again, there was recognition of my pain when he said that I have a 'much higher coping capacity' than most and that people like me just keep going until we can't do it anymore. He told the story of a footballer whom everyone had viewed as very strong and thought would always be okay. I knew who he meant: former AFL player Danny Frawley's car ran off the road, hit a tree and he died. Many believe he took his own life. My GP was also pleased to hear that I was going to see a psychiatrist and was interested to know what the outcome would be.

My husband has also commented on how I put it out there that I am strong and can cope, and that since I generally do, people just expect it of me. My naturopath agrees and has noted that people also expect more of me than others. Another interesting observation was made by an acquaintance when discussing the illness of depression. He wondered whether depression happens when a person is at a crossroads in their life and that it therefore has a function. It comes when change is needed. That was certainly the case in September 2021, if not in May 2022.

Psychology is a broad field, and my next appointment in Dandenong exemplified that. This session had three main themes – being strong, the metaphysical and feeling let down by a mental health service. I surprised myself when I brought the metaphysical into it, but clearly it is important to me. In the context of my reluctance to engage in help-seeking behaviours, I spoke about my near-death experience and the resulting belief that my life was going to be hard. I recalled a conversation in that near-death experience with my spirit guides in which I stated that I thought I could handle it. G had been concerned about my belief that life was always going to be hard. It felt good explaining the reason for that belief, especially in a non-judgemental environment.

With the psychologist being open-minded, I was emboldened and revealed my belief that an entity that I now believe was my violent father in my past life had tried to get to me in this life. It was many years ago, but having heard this, she queried whether I'd ever had psychodynamic therapy, as this could be a good fit for me. I have long been interested in psychodynamic therapy[5] and felt a strange sense of empowerment by knowing that someone else understood. We agreed that we would both look for someone suitable for future sessions beyond what Monash Health could provide.

On 16 June, I consulted with the psychiatrist at Monash Health, having already given a copy of my summary of my antidepressant withdrawal journal to the mental health team there. This history formed part of the discussion with me, making it clear that I did not want to be on them. I wanted an alternative psychiatric medication that was sustainable. My naturopath will retire one day, and I will not have the same relationship with another one. Seeing Mum and Dad go into a nursing home had also made me think. Dr T was easy to talk to and thorough as we explored my history with depression. He saw echoes of bipolar there but said we would have known if I was bipolar by now, so it is recurrent depressive disorder – or depressive episodes periodically throughout the lifespan.[6] He pointed out that while anyone can have a depressive episode, this is not true of bipolar. Bipolar always runs in families. Therefore, given my family history and the fact that my son has it, I do have some of the genes.

This was a good consultation. We had covered a lot of ground, and I felt heard and respected. Importantly, Dr T noted that people like me sometimes respond better to bipolar medication (that is, mood stabilisers) rather than antidepressants. It was worth a try. The plan was to commence with taking a low dose of quetiapine and titrate up to 100 mg while simultaneously tapering off the zopiclone. Quetiapine is quite sedating so it would cover the short-lived withdrawal of the zopiclone. I could resume tapering off the citalopram and work to get off the melatonin under the supervision of my GP. Later, I decided to stay on 10 mg of citalopram as I'm tired of the struggle. That dose has not caused me to require higher doses of melatonin so I'm confident that staying on it won't cause me any future issues.

I felt good about the medication change and discussed this at length with G at our next psychology session on 20

June. Since it had been a big issue for me, we also explored the issue with the long-term acquaintance whose comments earlier in the year had hurt me. By not being able to say that my son is disabled, a fact of life for me, she also effectively dismissed thirty years of looking after him. Apparently, she has never accepted him for who he is. That this comment came when I was approaching burnout explains why it had such an impact. I decided that I can accept that at times she is just clueless, that she has no filter, but it is *not* okay to just gloss over me being a caregiver. I can't tiptoe around this. It is integral to my sense of self.

However, my role as a caregiver was about to change, as a phone call from my NDIS support coordinators revealed the exciting news that a house was available in East Cranbourne for Jason, and that they were willing to take him. David and I inspected the house and met the coordinator on Monday 27 June and loved both. On the strength of the coordinator, whom I liked immediately, and following a prompt from our support coordinator, we decided to jump in and let Jason have an overnight stay the following weekend.

I delivered the exciting news when I saw my psychologist that afternoon in Dandenong. The other two main themes were my relationship with my parents and the importance of *not* being their caregiver, and what I would do should I become suicidal again. The latter was strongly reinforced as attempted suicide cannot be taken lightly. It is known that a second attempt is more likely in the weeks and months following the first, and it had only been a month.

Later that week, I visited Dandenong again for my follow-up appointment with Dr T, the psychiatrist. We did a recap of what the psychologist and I had been working on, as well as discussing my progress in terms of the medication change. All was going well. No need to see him again. I was certainly happy to be getting off the zopiclone. The endless merry-go-round of trying to get off antidepressants, so I could taper off the melatonin and eventually the sleeping tablets, had become a source of frustration. It had been going on for more than twelve years. Now I had been able to reduce the melatonin from 10 mg to 5 mg, given the sedation of the quetiapine, so things were looking up in that department. Finally!

With the improvement of my mood and general outlook, my next psychology appointment had been scheduled for two weeks after the previous one, with a view to making it my last. G had a cold, so we converted to a telehealth session. The themes in and of themselves reflected a distinct shift. Instead of my thoughts closing in on me, as they had been a few weeks earlier, they were now opening up. I wanted to know if I would recover from the caregiver burnout, conceptualising myself as a cat retreating to lick its wounds. G pointed out that if people didn't recover, professionals would be leaving their jobs in their droves. It therefore seems likely that recovery is on the horizon. This is important because caring about and for others is part of the mothering energy that is integral to who I am, and I wouldn't want to lose that. G believes that I will find a niche somewhere as a volunteer, as I have a lot to give. It was encouraging to hear this.

Medication-wise, I had already felt the quetiapine kicking in, despite not yet being on the full dose of 100 mg. My thinking was clearer, sharper, I was more motivated, and I definitely felt brighter. There was much to look forward to. This was a sharp contrast from just a few weeks earlier. G made sure I was aware of who to contact should I become suicidal again, reminded me to use my writing to identify the need to ask for help, and we ended my final consultation with Monash Health. It had been a good session.

Meanwhile, I had been in contact with a new, private psychologist who offered an appointment for Monday 18 July. G planned to contact him and do a handover which I felt would be good. He would have the background of what we had worked on. My plan was to use future sessions to delve into some deeper issues, such as past-life emotional breakthroughs and how the past influences me in the present.

My brother had kept me informed about Mum and Dad's care and in July, I finally went to visit Mum. Dad's section of the aged care centre was in lockdown, so sadly I was unable to see him. Nonetheless, visiting Mum purely as her daughter, not a caregiver, was a positive and enjoyable experience. Our relationship had changed. I had established a boundary, and it felt good. I enjoyed the visit.

Deeper healing would be the goal of my future psychodynamic therapy, but for now I felt I was able to draw a line under the immediacy of both my suicidal crisis of 2021 and my attempted suicide of May 2022. I was beginning to look to the future again. A healthy outlook. I was recovering.

*

'Depression is a serious illness. You need to take it seriously.' This is what the Casey CATT psychiatrist told me in May 2021. I didn't disagree. I just didn't agree that I needed antidepressants. When I didn't agree, he became frustrated and asked what I wanted him to do for me. Listening would have been a good start. Validating me and looking for another option would have been a good path to take. *I needed to be taken seriously.* At my naturopath's rooms, I was, so I went back there.

The messaging given to mental health patients is important. When a person is unwell, their struggle needs to be recognised and validated. The last thing they need is to be told they are strong. We are people; I am a person. I need help too, regardless of how strong you might think I am. Listen to me.

Thanks to a psychiatrist who did listen, I now understand that I have bipolar genes in me and that people like me sometimes respond better to bipolar medication, such as mood stabilisers, than antidepressants. The depression is said to be different. Bipolar people are also fast serotonin processors, something my naturopath said about me many years ago. The body needs serotonin to make melatonin. Somehow, the action of antidepressants in me impedes that. Nonetheless, it is now clear that I am in that small percentage of people for whom psychiatric drugs do help. Apparently, I have just been on the wrong ones.

Be it taking antidepressants, being told I am strong or being interrupted during a medical consultation, my story is one of a person whose struggles were not taken seriously. I am only one person, and it doesn't matter how strong I am. I have a mental illness, and there are times when I need help. Depression is definitely a serious illness and health professionals need to take it seriously. Not doing so can cost lives. It almost cost me mine.

CHAPTER 5

Therapy insights and changed spirituality

Caregiving and the 'id'

Caregiving, paid or unpaid, is hard work. In my experience, considering my thirty-two-year journey as the primary caregiver of my son who has multiple disabilities and a mental health issue, unpaid carers are often very strong people who work extremely hard. Outside the worlds of disability, mental health, aged care etc., however, their struggles are often disenfranchised, poorly understood and easily dismissed by others. Being strong only serves to hide the emotional pain, the physical and mental exhaustion and the difficulties of the caregiver's daily existence. It becomes a shield against the unthinkable alternative – not being able to cope and crumbling, leaving the person needing care alone and unsupported. It's not surprising, then, that in the face of enormous, sustained, caregiving pressure, together with other psycho-social stressors, some caregivers like me suffer caregiver burnout.

Burnout doesn't happen overnight. In my case, I had been feeling the weight of my role since Jason transitioned onto the NDIS in mid-2018. There was increased paperwork, the need for me to coordinate Jason's supports and manage the allotted budget, along with the existing personal care and other daily caring duties. When Jason spent a week in Adelaide in November 2019, participating in a sporting tournament with the aid of a one-to-one carer, I enjoyed the freedom from the workload so much that I didn't really want him to come home. I didn't want to admit that to myself. He is my son, and I love him, so how could I feel this way?

At that time, I was diagnosed with acute stress reaction and was already writing that I was 'tired of always being the strong one ... [and that I] ... don't want to do it anymore', that I was feeling 'weighed down by the burden of being a caregiver, always giving to others, while pining to be nurtured for myself'. That was eighteen months before Mum became unwell, two and a half years before I was diagnosed with caregiver burnout.

It was hard balancing my deep desire to be free of being a caregiver with my natural desire to help others. I still enjoyed casual opportunities to counsel others, though I couldn't register as a counsellor and set up my own practice. It was even harder during Covid and with the additional demands of working with my brother to support my elderly parents who ultimately transitioned from living independently to being residents in an aged care facility. As much as I have long sought to balance the competing demands of caring for Jason with living my own life and enjoying activities purely for my own pleasure, the circumstances of 2019 to May 2022 simply did not allow for this. My life was not in balance at all. Indeed, during 2021 and most of 2022, I didn't even know what I enjoyed doing anymore, let alone how to go about it.

In psychoanalytic terms, I was no longer in touch with my 'id' (the Freudian concept of the rash, impulsive, pleasure-seeking drive within), something my therapist picked up on very early in our sessions. Caregiving may be intrinsic to who I am – I do enjoy supporting and helping others – but nurturing myself and doing things for the sheer pleasure of it is important for my wellbeing too; hedonism, rather than the vicarious joy experienced from caring for others.

That there was a conflict resulting from these two competing themes – the burden of caregiving as opposed to experiencing pleasure from the spontaneity of helping others – only made it harder. The weight of responsibility pulled me down and didn't allow me to express myself in ways that I find uplifting, as I had done when volunteering as a telephone counsellor with Griefline. Was helping others the only thing that made me happy?

If the 'id' is the child within, I had lost my relationship *with* that child. It was as though that little girl had been taken from me without my consent, and that no contact was allowed, as if the courts had made a ruling against me. I could only operate from the standpoint of my 'superego' – the moral conscience of my being, which lent itself to the sense of caregiving duty that I felt. There was no other option. If there was, I was unaware of what it might be. I felt imprisoned in an endless, daily grind of caregiving without end – a caregiving role I was rapidly coming to resent. Who cared for me?

Burnout and suicide

The burnout revealed itself when, as is so eloquently described by Sam Dylan Finch,[7] my 'capacity for emotional pain [had] outweighed the amount of time [I was] able to wait for relief, at the same moment when [I had] access to the means to end [my] life.' I was exhausted and could not control the suicidal thoughts any longer. I took an overdose. It was, as Finch says, 'the ultimate state of burnout'.

Finch further points out that, 'in order to attempt suicide a person has to be in the neurological state where they can override their own survival instincts'. This explains my use of the psychological defence mechanism of dissociation. The ego fears death so the psyche separates – or disconnects – action from feeling as though the person is observing rather than actively participating in the suicide attempt. Clearly, the person attempting is conflicted, and I was no exception.

In one sense, as discussed with my therapist, it wasn't about survival – it was about embracing death. I didn't want to be here. Yet my ego feared death, so I, whoever that was spiritually or psychologically, had to override that fear in order to swallow the pills. In doing so and surviving, I was then forced to confront the many psychological, and indeed spiritual, conflicts this brought to the surface, not all of them in or of the present.

That Christmas of 1972 when I experienced my near-death experience, I believe there were spiritual reasons why I had not died. Though I am unable to remember them, I have always felt comfortable with my decision to return to this life, knowing that I had work to do and that my time would come. For that reason, death was no longer something to be feared but the *act* of dying was, so I banished it from my thoughts and got on with the business of living.

In the months following my suicide attempt, while reading a book entitled *God I Am*,[8] I became intrigued with the concept of a 'oneness', in particular the idea that 'in order to remember oneness, survival thinking has to be surrendered'. My near-death experience had altered my perception and given me a sense of the interconnectedness of all living things. Was I now remembering 'oneness'? Are these the same concepts? One can never be certain when searching for the answers to such profound questions but taking the pills has certainly changed the way I view death and dying.

Addressing the past

Death and dying are not just in the here and now. They involve deep philosophical questions along with a desire to explore profound questions about our mortality and for some, the possibility of a continuation of life after death. One seeks an assurance that life has meaning and that when confronted with death, a life lived has not been in vain.

My suicide attempt prompted a need to explore what I believe to have been a past life and its impact on me in the present. I was aware that relevant issues had been increasingly entering my consciousness, and now I wanted to deal with them and, hopefully, lay them to rest. While in a suicidal state, I had hidden behind what I call 'the façade of being strong' and used it as a 'shield protecting my core belief of always having to fight for my survival alone'. My therapist helped me to unpack this profound statement, and together we identified four powerful elements that underpinned it.

The façade of being strong and using it as a shield is a

psychological defence mechanism. I hide behind my strength, not wanting to feel the emotional pain. When I do feel the pain, I convert it into defensive anger. The greater the pain, the more intense the anger. In terms of survival, if I feel threatened, I can convert my fear of being hurt into anger and thus prepare my body to fight. This makes sense in light of a past life in which I was the victim of severe domestic violence.

Similarly, my core belief of always having to fight for my survival alone could reasonably be attributed to my past-life experiences. My mother from that time wasn't strong enough to stand up to my father, and I had tried to be the strong one. When it came to direct physical attacks on me, my only defence was the physical strength I could muster. No one came to my aid. At this point in time, I can only speculate, but it is reasonable to think that I had suffered repeated beatings from my alcohol-affected and violent father. I had to be strong. At times, I had to fight for my very survival – alone.

This core belief came with me into my present life. In exploring the following with my therapist, I gained clarity on just how deeply entrenched this belief was. When I was a child and experienced acute appendicitis on Christmas Day of 1972, the pain had been excruciating, yet I had told no one that I was actually in pain. When the family returned from visiting my paternal grandparents, picked me up from my maternal grandparents' house and took me home, I had felt so bad that I just wanted to lie on my bed. My actions in pushing my sister off my bed were uncharacteristic and alerted Mum and Dad to the fact that something was very wrong. Now, in the present, I asked myself if I would have held back from seeking help long enough to have inadvertently brought about my own death. After a period of contemplation, the answer was yes. A second related question then arose: would my vulnerable side have overridden the strong one to prevent a sense of abandonment and ensure my very survival? This time, the answer was no.

In exploring these two significant questions, my therapist helped me to see how my unconscious had been protecting me in the present. In my past life, I couldn't let anyone know that I was vulnerable because it wasn't safe. Asking for help would, most likely, have led to a beating. In order to survive, I had to use the façade of being strong, probably on a regular basis. It was a learned behaviour.

A fear of abandonment was also something I had learned, it seems, in that past life, and this is another reason why I couldn't tell anyone that I was in immense pain in 1972. In my past life, my mother had not been strong enough to stand up to my violent father, and I felt abandoned. She was not in the room with me when I died; she had not been there to protect me. It is possible that my fear of abandonment is the reason why, in this life, I tend to keep people at arm's length.

I can't be abandoned if no one gets close to me – another learned behaviour.

Thus far, psychodynamic therapy had helped me to identify some very powerful unconscious defence mechanisms that I was employing to protect my ego while simultaneously also almost bringing about my death by my own hand. By identifying these defence mechanisms, I was able to let my repressed feelings come to the surface and process them. In late October 2022, five months after my attempt at taking my own life, I suddenly realised that I am *not* alone. I am safe in the universe.

I had previously recognised this in 2017, following regular yoga practice and writing a piece about the traumatic grief I'd experienced from the failure of IVF some twenty-five years earlier. I experienced a profound recognition that:

- I don't have to be a caregiver anymore.
- I don't have to be strong for other people anymore.
- It is okay to feel [emotional] pain.
- It is okay to ask for help.
- I don't have to fight for my survival alone!

In addition, like an epiphany, I realised that:
- I am not alone.
- I am safe in the universe.
- I am one with the universe (oneness/ interconnectedness).

It wasn't just about being in this life or fearing death; it was about transcending that and seeing this life as one part of my overall existence, knowing that 'I' will still exist when my physical body is gone. Not just a belief in reincarnation, as before, but knowing that my spiritual being is of a higher consciousness and understanding the impermanence of material possessions. It was a profound shift from being a human being having a spiritual experience to a spiritual being having a human experience.

The dual issues of safety and abandonment apparently arising from my past life went deeper than previously discussed. It was not just that my arms couldn't protect me; I also experienced intense anger at the man who had actually beaten his own son (I was a boy in that life) to death. How could someone do that to their own child? No wonder I didn't feel I could let people in on my pain in this life. It simply didn't feel safe. I did, however, discover a technique for dealing with my anger at the man who had done this to me. I changed the narrative in my head. Instead of curling up in a foetal ball on my bed and trying to protect myself from the violence, I turned and faced my father before pushing him out the window where he plummeted to the ground below. With this simple change in thinking, I took back the power and erased victimhood. He would not hurt me again.

Yet, I recall trying to be 'good' and wanting to help my

abusive father. At some level, I guess I wanted to gain his approval. I can only speculate, but it is reasonable to think that I had some sort of attachment to him, perhaps the same anxious, insecure attachment I have exhibited in the present. I want to be loved, but I don't know how.

It wasn't safe for my mother in that life either. If she had tried to intervene, he would have turned on her and inflicted the same brutal punishment. The survival instinct is strong, and I guess she was no exception in wanting to preserve her own life. Nonetheless her inaction, her unwillingness or inability to stand up to him and fight for me – to protect me – meant that she had abandoned me to my fate. Mothers are supposed to protect their children. Mine didn't, and the penalty was death.

That very theme came up again in the present life when I was actively planning my own suicide in September 2021. I have written about this elsewhere so suffice it to say that the profound experience of my present-life mother intervening in a spiritual way while being unwell herself was more healing than I had realised at the time. She did what my mother in my past life didn't do – she protected me and saved me. I would definitely have attempted suicide without her intervention and, who knows, I may well have succeeded.

A corollary of the safety aspect here is the psychological defence mechanism of transference. This occurs when a person unconsciously transfers feelings about one person onto an entirely separate individual. My issues around safety were multi-layered. Consciously, I had attempted to take my own life and needed someone to protect me and prevent me from doing so again. That my current life mother had done what my past-life mother hadn't had not prevented me from taking an overdose some eight months later. Clearly, I was still struggling with the issue of safety, and this manifested in me feeling an emotional attachment to my GP that I'd never felt in the thirty-odd years I'd known him.

It was early June 2022, just days after I had taken the overdose. I had gone to see him to get a mental health plan as recommended by the CATT team. When he realised what I'd done, his immediate response was, 'That's not like you'. That simple comment elicited a powerful response from me. Not only did I feel that the depth of my pain was heard and validated, but his words demonstrated to me that he cared, while simultaneously making me feel safe. He was going to take care of me.

I recognised the transference but didn't understand why it was happening until some weeks later. It began in early June, and I noticed the effect weakening in late October when, following a powerful session with my therapist, I experienced a breakthrough. In the epiphany, I realised I no longer had to fight for my survival alone. I was safe in the universe, regardless of my mortality. I didn't need my GP to make me feel safe anymore. I was going to be okay. The psychodynamic therapy was working.

Perhaps my transference onto my GP served a second purpose as well. Feeling that he genuinely cared about me meant I could contain my fears of abandonment. He was doing what my mother in my past life had not been able to do – he was working to keep me safe.

Complex relationships

In psychodynamic and perhaps metaphysical terms (reincarnation), it makes sense that David and I have come together in this life. In my husband's case, I can clearly see now that he has an avoidant-attachment style (Bowlby, 1969).[9] This does not make him a bad person, not at all. I just believe that he was the past-life mother who did not have the resources to prevent my past-life father from inflicting horrific physical abuse on me as her son. Being his equal rather than his/her child has allowed me to continue in my role as the 'strong' one, without needing to also be the protector/carer that I tried to be in my past life. That I have also wanted to be protected, while simultaneously being strong, has caused issues in our marriage. It has led to me feeling let down and abandoned, a theme David has not yet been unable to comprehend or correct. (He also struggles to believe in reincarnation, but that is part of his journey, and I cannot interfere.)

In this life, there are differences in how we were both raised. David's family were good people, but they didn't exhibit the physical or emotional warmth and love that I had experienced growing up. Indeed, I had always wanted physical affection and emotional love from a life partner, but it has not been forthcoming.

Indeed, in relating the marital difficulties and discord of recent years to my therapist, he has been able to help me to understand the importance of roles. Sometimes people are just in the wrong role, for example, being a lover instead of a friend. If we change the role, it works better.

Our marriage had broken down late in 2018 and it had been an on-again, off-again struggle since then. The stresses of caring for Jason, with his multiple disabilities, during a global pandemic only served to put more pressure on a relationship that simply wasn't working. By the time we took Jason on a family cruise in December 2022 – likely to be the last of our family holidays – I had reached the point where I couldn't keep up the charade any longer. I couldn't keep living a lie. I'm fond of David, but I can't be in a romantic relationship with him anymore. Having talked it through, David and I both agreed that being friends while still living together was worth a try. He doesn't want me to leave, and I don't want to go. Safety, security and stability are all important to me. Even as a teenager, I was in no rush to move out and live independently, unlike many of my peers.

Redefining the relationship has also lifted the weight of expectation from my shoulders. I can't feel let down or abandoned if he is my friend and not my romantic partner. I expect less from him. Equally, I'm not so demanding of him. While struggling with depression, powerful grief and suicidal ideation in 2021, I put him through an impossible time during which he could not say or do anything right. I regret that. He is a good man, and he didn't deserve it. But I guess, as burnout was approaching, I really resented having to care for him, instead of the other way around. Nonetheless, we work well as a team and can cohabit without too many issues so, hopefully, we have found a workable solution. Time will tell.

The complexity of my current and past-life relationship with my husband is also mirrored in my lack of effective help-seeking behaviours. Being strong has been a constant for me, but by late May 2022, it was no longer serving me well. Not being able to be vulnerable – to be exposed to possible physical or emotional attacks or harm – meant that I used defensive anger and projection to avoid the unwanted feelings. In the projection, I put high expectations on myself and thus have the same expectations of others. My belief has been that they should know how I'm feeling when, in fact, they don't. It's a detour: I put on to others what I don't want to feel myself. It seems therefore that I expected my husband to know how I was feeling, and got angry with him when he didn't. This was totally unfair on him, especially during 2021, and it didn't help me either.

A comment by a long-term acquaintance about my disabled son being 'different' also hit a nerve. It was very hurtful, and my anger was intense. Did I also expect her to know how I would feel when she disenfranchised thirty years of hard work in raising and caring for him? I think I did. I think it is reasonable to expect people to have accepted my situation, given that it had been twenty-eight years since his autism diagnosis. Nevertheless, I was approaching burnout at the time and may have reacted more strongly, given the emotional pain I was apparently working to avoid – that I no longer wanted to be my son's primary caregiver.

Intensive short-term dynamic psychotherapy (ISTDP)

That I have used various unconscious psychological defence mechanisms to avoid emotional pain is not unusual. Everyone does this. It's just that we are not aware we are doing it! In my case projection, transference, dissociation and the façade of being strong have all acted to protect my psyche from anything it perceives as anxiety-provoking, and thus a threat. In my case, the issue of safety appears to have been a major driver in my unconscious use of these defence mechanisms, until life became so overwhelming that I overrode my fears of being unsafe and attempted to take my own life.

According to the Philosophy and Theory of ISTDP – ISTDP Australia website, 'we can develop a tendency to pull away from intimacy which results in us becoming disconnected from our own feelings'. I have always kept people at arm's length, although I didn't know why. I know that I don't know how to let someone love me, even though I have yearned for that to happen. Importantly, it prevents me 'from being able to feel cared for by others'.

ISTDP aims to assist 'the patient to overcome his or her own internal struggles with his or her feelings and emotions about past and present experiences that overwhelm him or her due to their frightening, threatening or painful nature'.[10]

In exploring the past and present influences on me in the present, it has become clear that the need for safety, while being unable to be truly intimate with another human being, has greatly hampered my marital relations. In addition, I have been employing another defence mechanism to protect my psyche from anxiety-provoking and very painful feelings with the use of control. During what I now call the 'IVF years' (1995–1999), my psyche had presented me with a powerful visual symbol, a cubic gift box wrapped with a ribbon, tied in a bow. This was the repository for all my unwanted feelings. I needed to contain and thus control them.

The traumatic experience in 2019 when my husband was in a serious car accident saw me dissociating and employing the defence mechanism of control. Consciously, I was angry at David because I was trying to decide whether to end the marriage and didn't want my choice taken from me. I had felt helpless during the IVF years and couldn't bear the idea of feeling that way again, so I sought control over my situation. It is now clear to me that I use control to avoid being vulnerable.

I also employed the same mechanism in 2019 to contain my unwanted feelings about my marriage. I put my weddings rings, that are welded together, into a thimble and under a cover. In this context, containment was control. I kept my rings there until I felt more comfortable about staying in the marriage. That said, control used as a tool to manage anxiety (that is, problem solving to manage a situation) can be differentiated from the control that acts to avoid unwanted feelings. Knowing the roads you will take to get you to your destination, before getting in the car and departing, makes sense and is perfectly normal.

The defence mechanisms uncovered in therapy all point to one major thing – that, for me, being truly vulnerable is frightening. In my past life, safety was the major issue, safety in order to survive. Being overtly afraid was apparently not productive, so I learned not to show such feelings. I learned to put up a façade of being strong and to use it as a shield, a defensive 'strategy' that I brought with me into the present life.

A concomitant issue is that of helplessness. Being helpless means being vulnerable and having to face my fears. Not having learned to do that in my past life, I found it difficult in this life too, especially when I had always wanted to have children and raise them well. At an unconscious level, possibly even subconscious, I wanted to break the cycle of domestic abuse. I did not want to be the perpetrator of domestic violence. I saw this as the most valuable contribution I could make to this world and was devastated when I couldn't make it happen.

Studying psychology gave me a new dream and I began to seriously consider doing a Master's degree and getting fully qualified. I had to surrender that dream to the harsh reality of my son developing bipolar disorder II amid expectations of myself that were impossibly high. Later, I commenced putting my copious written material – writing being my emotional release – into my life story. (Maybe one day, someone might read it. Who knows?) I don't feel the need now, however, to finish it or to replace it with another dream. The reasons for this are more spiritual than material. It is when we go through the hardest times in our lives that we grow the most spiritually, and this time period is no exception.

Spiritual growth

In addition to psychodynamic therapy, my therapist works with the Eastern practice and philosophy of mindfulness. On more than one occasion, he had me close my eyes, focus on my body and seek to identify what emotions it was holding. Early on in our sessions, I identified anger, which led to a discussion about the whole 'being strong' issue. On another occasion, I became very peaceful and felt the 'I am' of Eastern philosophies inhabiting my heart space. As Erbe states, 'The soul remembers, the intellect does not'.[11] This led to a conversation about spirituality and the discovery that we both have very similar beliefs. That we do helped on more than one occasion during our sessions.

The practice of mindfulness was encouraged on several occasions, specifically to focus on the space between what I have realised intellectually and how I feel; to let myself *feel*. In addition, since I am a spiritual person, it was suggested that I need to spend more time focusing on the heart chakra area. According to my therapist, I am good with the intellect (third eye to neck) and action (the navel area) but need to spend more time in-between. This is also in accordance with me needing to be in touch with my 'id' and allow my playful self to re-emerge, as mentioned earlier in this chapter.

By allowing my feelings to come into my consciousness, I can sit with them, then allow them to disperse. I'm told this is the way to disperse the karma. A corollary of this, of course, is to free myself as much as possible from the attachment to things and the material world. As my therapist pointed out, in Buddhism, the philosophy is that we create our own suffering. We need to keep coming back to the 'I am'. This sentiment is also mentioned in *God I Am*[12] which notes, 'there is only one possession we have to surrender and that is the sum total of all our anxieties'.

On one occasion during our sessions, my therapist and I departed from clinical psychology and talked about what I now see as a partial Kundalini awakening[13] that I experienced in April 1989. At that time, troubled by many stressors, I found myself on my knees with tears streaming down my face, and – being a Christian at the time – repenting and giving my all to Jesus. For the next month, I experienced the most overwhelming, powerful love that words simply cannot describe. My therapist commented that giving our all is what we need to do – to surrender ourselves completely. He then told me about a thirteenth-century mystic named Rumi who said, 'You have to keep breaking your heart until it opens'. Was this what was happening to me? Possibly, since the same sentiment is mentioned by Erbe: 'once a human being learns to look beyond his physical needs and opens his heart aspect, learning begins.'[14]

Of course, it's hard to be certain when one is faced with

such profound concepts, but I resonated strongly with this line in *God I Am*: 'In order to remember Oneness, survival thinking has to be surrendered.'[15] If I didn't remember oneness following my near-death experience in 1972 or in 1989, I did now.

As already stated, I had transcended my fear of death and was now viewing my life as one part of my overall existence, part of the *samsara*, the wheel of life as described in Eastern philosophy, part of the 'one'. Caregiver burnout had, then, led to a profound transformation in spiritual beliefs that sustain me in everyday life. As Joe Dispenza[16] has said, 'experience leads to knowledge, which then leads to wisdom.'

Causes of burnout

Certainly, I had experienced an incredibly difficult period in my life in which everything had seemed out of balance. Since the IVF years, I had pursued ways of supporting others. I studied psychology, dreamed of becoming a therapist, volunteered as a telephone counsellor with Griefline and continued finding ways of giving, even when I was unable to work, outside of my role as my son's primary caregiver. All was well as I do enjoy, as my therapist noted, expressing myself by giving to others spontaneously.

But things changed. Jason's transition onto the NDIS created a lot of work for me, something I resented because it was all left to me, and I had no choice. My husband retired from the workforce and the schisms in our relationship that I knew were there began to manifest on a daily basis. The horror year of 2019 in which he and Jason were involved in separate car accidents and the financial issues related to our investment property put even more pressure on our marriage and left me feeling like the weight of responsibility was primarily mine to bear. David did pull his weight, at least with the property, but I still felt that he needed reassurance, meaning that I needed to be the strong one. Again.

At an unconscious level, this would have resonated with my core belief that I always had to fight for my survival alone, but I didn't know that then. I just wanted someone to hold me and tell me that everything was going to be all right. I now know that we both unconsciously feared for our safety and wanted the other to provide it, a dynamic that was never going to work.

My husband is on his own journey, but I now feel safe in the universe and part of the oneness. The work that my therapist and I have done in uncovering the importance of safety to me, along with the profound changes in my spirituality, mean that I no longer need or expect my life partner to protect me when my arms couldn't, and to be someone he is not. I can remove the unfair expectations I had of him. Changing roles, from that of romantic partners to friends, also seems to be working. From my perspective, I feel a greater sense of balance in the relationship. Our living environment is a stable and safe one for both of us.

I still, as my therapist puts it, 'have a desire to express myself – to be who I really am – like giving to others spontaneously', and it does need to be spontaneous. I suffered caregiver burnout and I no longer want to be tied to a caregiving role. I want to be free, to not always be strong, but to be who I truly am.

*

I entered therapy seeking answers to the profound issues surrounding death and dying that my suicide attempt had brought into my consciousness. I had carried past-life trauma into the present and, in the abyss of suicidality, coupled with a diagnosis of caregiver burnout, there was a need for the unconscious to be made conscious and to be processed. Brief psychodynamic therapy, which aims for self-awareness and understanding of the influence of the past on present behaviour, was a good fit for me.

Attempting to take my own life, in which I had to override my own survival instincts[17] had opened the proverbial Pandora's box, itself perhaps an indication of containment and thus control, and saw me drowning in a plethora of existential questions. Discovering the psychological defence mechanisms I had apparently developed in a past life also helped me to gain clarity in the present. The ego fears death, yet I had died, so it continued to protect my psyche from the painful, unwanted experience of me being truly vulnerable, even in the present life. The conundrum, and perhaps therefore the psychic conflicts, was that it was no longer working. So where to now?

Of course, psychodynamic therapy deals with unconscious processes so the answers to my existential questions could not be found there, despite the undoubted efficacy of the restructuring of my psychological defence system and improvement in my anxiety regulation. I feel more able to be vulnerable and to let others in, which was a key therapy goal from the outset.

Nonetheless, it was the shared beliefs of my therapist and me that helped me to clarify the existential and spiritual that means so much to me. In transcending fears of death and seeing my mortality as just one component of my overall existence, I have rediscovered 'oneness'.[18]

Life is about many things, including experience to gain knowledge and then wisdom.[19] Life learning includes understanding that attachment causes suffering and that we need to keep coming back to the 'I am'. Ultimately, I have learned that I am strong, but not invincible. I am also vulnerable.

In fact, I just am.

Endnotes

1. LA Pervin & OP John, *Personality: Theory and Research*. 8th ed., John Wiley and Sons, New York, 2001.
2. National Library of Medicine, Screening for Depression in Adults and Older Adults in Primary Care: An Updated Systematic Review, https://www.ncbi.nlm.nih.gov/books/NBK36406/table/ch1.t2/#:~:text=First%2Dgeneration,Nortriptyline%2C%20Amoxapine%2C%20Protriptyline%2C%20Trimipramine, accessed 8 May 2021
3. Community and Family Services | Grief Counselling | Counselling Helpline (griefline.org.au), accessed 2 March 2023
4. Caregiver Burnout: Symptoms and Treatment (healthline.com), accessed 2 March 2023
5. Psychodynamic therapy is based on the psychoanalysis originally developed by Sigmund Freud and focuses on unconscious processes as they are manifested in the client's current behaviour. It aims for self-awareness and understanding of the influence of the past on present behaviour. See National Library of Medicine, Brief Interventions and Brief Therapies for substance Abuse, Chapter 7, Brief Psychodynamic Therapy, https://www.ncbi.nlm.nih.gov/books/NBK64952/, accessed 8 May 2023

6   What Is Recurrent Major Depressive Disorder? (overlandiop.com), accessed 2 March 2023
7   Sam Dylan Finch, accessed 23 January 2023
8   PO Erbe, *God I Am: From Tragic to Magic*, 2nd ed., Triad Publishers, Cairns, Australia, 1991.
9   J Bowlby, *Attachment and loss, Vol. I: Attachment*, Basic Books, New York, 1969.
10 Intensive Short–Term Dynamic Psychotherapy (goodtherapy.org) – accessed 20 February 2023
11 *ibid.*
12 *ibid.*
13 In Hinduism, Kundalini refers to the fundamental life force said to be dormant in the *muladhara* or root chakra at the base of the spine. It can also be conceptualised as 'an aspect of Shakti, divine female energy, and the inseparable lover of Shiva, universal consciousness'. See also <u>Transformative Meditation & Yoga Retreats | Hridaya Yoga (hridaya-yoga.com)</u>, accessed 2 May 2023
14 *Intensive Short–Term Dynamic Psychotherapy (goodtherapy.org)*
15 *ibid.*
16 The Official Website of Dr Joe Dispenza: Unlimited with Dr Joe Dispenza, accessed 23 February 2023
17 Sam Dylan Finch, *ibid.*
18 Erbe, *ibid*
19 The Official Website of Dr Joe Dispenza, *ibid.*

www.ingramcontent.com/pod-product-compliance
Lightning Source LLC
Chambersburg PA
CBHW030042100526
44590CB00011B/296